God's Love Is Forever

Daniel James Duke

Published by Delinea Publishing, 2024.

For my children and grandchildren

Foreword

Daily devotionals fill the shelves of physical and virtual bookstores. Sincere God-seekers as far back as the ninth century A.D. have attempted to shape and guide the deepening of individual religious faith through daily, dedicated morning or evening time for scripture reading, self-reflection, and quiet prayer. Devotionals come in all sizes, for various time periods, focus, events, and purposes, and for different people and professions. Well-known celebrity-pastors produce them, churches and ministries promote them, and individuals publish them. Devotionals are a useful way to structure time spent with the Word of God and to enhance our prayer lives. A good devotional is like an instruction booklet: the step-by-step information on the pages - perhaps even a solution for whatever challenge required the instruction booklet in the first place - guides us in preparing for time with the Father.

God's Love is Forever is not just the title of this instruction book, it is the founding principle of Christianity. It is the essence of Jesus Christ and his message. Jesus's entire ministry was love. It is the Good News. God's love is always worth examining and reflecting upon, and it is always worth acting upon. This instruction booklet guides readers through daily reflections on God's love: for us, for the world, for each other, and for all times. The daily scripture, reflection, and prayer in each entry urges deeper engagement with the loving Father who welcomes, forgives, and comforts.

God's Love is Forever is a timely and helpful guide in this season of uncertainty, disunity, hatred, and fear. Amid the presence of evil, God reminds us He is an ever-present help and the constant source of all that is good. In Him and with Him, we will find peace, calm, and joy. This book will help deepen faith in God's love and inspire a closer walk with him. At the very least, it makes plain God's clear and persistent intent to love his children - despite our best efforts to run away from Him. This alone is worth a read.

I encourage you to keep *God's Love is Forever* close by, so that when you need a spiritual boost, you can reach for the book and find inspiration or consolation in its messages. And I also hope that the messages lead you to explore the referenced chapters and books of the Bible for additional insight and context. For now, I invite you to calm your spirit, turn to the next section, and begin your meditation on God's everlasting and unconditional love. May it bring you joy and peace.

Faith Churn-Smith
Senior Pastor
Zamar Worship Center & Ministries
https://zamarworshipctr.org/
Baltimore, MD

Acknowledgments

To my beloved wife, dear brother, caring sister-in-law, and supportive sister, in the presence of your unwavering love and unyielding support, the idea for a devotional blossomed into a labor of profound inspiration and commitment. With immense gratitude and heartfelt appreciation, I dedicate these words to each of you, for you have helped to guide this work to its completion.

To my cherished wife, your unflagging belief in my abilities and your constant encouragement have been the driving forces behind this journey. Your keen insights and thoughtful feedback have illuminated the path, leading me toward a deeper understanding of the message I seek to share. I dedicate this devotional to you, my pillar of strength and the beacon of light in my life.

To my dear brother, your invaluable input and astute observations have brought clarity to my thoughts and enriched the essence of this devotional. Your wisdom and understanding have been a source of inspiration, propelling me forward on this meaningful quest. I offer these pages to you, my brother, with boundless appreciation and love.

To my caring sister-in-law, your kindness and encouragement have infused this devotional with warmth and compassion. Your discerning eye and gentle guidance have played a pivotal role in shaping its essence. I dedicate this work to you as a token of gratitude for the generous support you have given me.

To my supportive sister, your enthusiasm and eagerness to listen have been a constant source of motivation. Your genuine interest in my journey has been a guiding light, illuminating the way during moments of doubt. With heartfelt gratitude, I dedicate this devotional to you, my sister, as a testament to the bond we share.

In the warmth of your love and gentleness of your guidance, I found the strength to share this devotional with the world. Together, we have woven a tapestry of support, turning mere words into a symphony of devotion. As I reflect upon my journey, I am humbled by the love and care you continuously shower upon me. Your presence in my life has added depth to my purpose, and your encouragement has fanned the fire of love in my soul.

With heartfelt dedication and deepest love,
Daniel

Introduction

This devotional is an instruction booklet. Created during Lent as personal daily reflections on scripture and prayer, these devotions transitioned from musings on my laptop to daily texts to my family. The topic was undeniably appealing to them, and my texts generated conversation and insights I had not expected. By all accounts, the daily devotions were a blessing to the group, and the idea for the book was born.

This edition includes scriptures from the English Standard and New International Versions of the Bible, with insights into their meaning and relevant prayers. The book also includes bonus material: an eight-day reflection on the Beatitudes, a key teaching from Jesus's early ministry and foundational scripture for Christians; an "any day" devotion, with scripture and reflections for any time you need the spirit; and a letter from God, a meditation on what God might say if he wrote you a letter. The messages in these reflections apply to any situation, any time, and any person. If you have a desire to nurture your love for God and align with his will, this book will provide you with daily scripture, reflections, and prayers to aid in your spiritual efforts.

As you read the devotions, let them open extra levels of spiritual development for you. Start them today and read them again when you finish. As often as you read them, your soul will respond in new and deeper ways. Keep these nearby and refer to them when you feel down, separated from God, or need to reconnect to the Source of all love.

Find a few minutes each day when you will not be interrupted and can be quiet. Do whatever you need to set the scene for a meeting with God. Light a candle, play music, write in a journal. No matter how, just reflect and pray.

D aniel Duke
      Assistant Pastor
Zamar Worship Center & Ministries
Baltimore, MD

GOD'S LOVE IS FOREVER

The Devotions

God's Everlasting Love

"The Lord appeared to us in the past, saying: 'I have loved you with an everlasting love; I have drawn you with unfailing kindness.'" Jeremiah 31:3

God loved humanity first, even before we grew to love Him. God's unconditional love and grace are central aspects of the Christian faith and encourage us to show love and kindness to others. God loves all people, and his unconditional love extends to all of us regardless of beliefs, actions, or circumstances. This wonderful, transcendent truth encourages us to love ourselves and each other more each day because we are worthy of His love.

Today's Prayer

Dear God, thank you for your unconditional love, which always surrounds and sustains me. Your love is the source of all life and the foundation of my existence. I know no matter what I do, you will always love and forgive me. Help me experience your love in a deeper way and share it with others. Teach me to love like you do - with patience, kindness, compassion, and mercy. I ask for your guidance and strength as I strive to live a life worthy of your love. I pray all these things in Jesus's name. Amen.

Unconditional and Available

"The Lord your God is with you, the Mighty Warrior who saves. He will take great delight in you; in his love he will no longer rebuke you, but will rejoice over you with singing." Zephaniah 3:17

God's love is unconditional and extends to all people, regardless of their beliefs, actions, backgrounds, or situations. God's love is always available to those who seek it, and through God's love, individuals can experience forgiveness, salvation, and fulfillment. Belief in God's healing love guides us to turn to him for comfort and support and to give our love and kindness to others, as they also receive God's love.

When you have hard feelings toward someone - a family member, spouse, friend, or yourself - take a moment to think about God's unconditional love for them. If the creator of the universe can find it in his spirit to love that person, can't you? Remind yourself that God takes delight in and no longer rebukes them. Focus your heart on God and pray for his love to consume and inspire you.

Today's Prayer

Dear Lord, I come to you today with a humble heart, filled with knowing that your love for me is unconditional. Your love is like no other, and I am so grateful for all you do for me every day. Thank you for your grace, mercy, and forgiveness. Thank you for your never-ending patience and for always being there for me, no matter what I do or say. Help me understand your love more fully and experience more deeply each day. Give me the strength to love others the same way that you love me: with patience, kindness, and selflessness. Thank you for your boundless love, and for the peace that comes with knowing that you cherish and love me forever. In Jesus's name, I pray. Amen.

God Loves Everyone

"**B**ut because of his great love for us, God, who is rich in mercy, made us alive with Christ even when we were dead in transgressions—it is by grace you have been saved." Ephesians 2:4-5

God's universal love is not dependent on any condition. It is not limited by a person's race, ethnicity, sexuality, gender, social status, beliefs, actions, or circumstances. God loves all people equally and without reservation. This principle encourages us to extend the same love, kindness, and understanding to others, regardless of how different they are from us. God's love is the fundamental message of hope, compassion, and inclusiveness, and it challenges us to act gently and benevolently toward others.

Social and news media and politicians perpetuate and exploit our differences. But Jesus was a uniter. He brought people together in ways that shocked the leaders of his community. He revealed his divinity to a woman considered unworthy by his own people. He dined with tax collectors, who were maligned by the Jewish leaders of his day. Jesus welcomed everyone to hear his message of love and forgiveness. He built bridges between the deep chasms that separated men and women, Jew and Gentile, rich and poor, and healthy and sick. To be sure we follow his example, Jesus gave the eleventh commandment: "A new commandment I give to you, that you love one another; as I have loved you, that you also love one another." John 13:34

Today's Prayer

Dear God, thank you for your boundless love that extends to all people. I am grateful for the love that never fails, never gives up, and never fades away. Help me embrace and internalize your love so I may share it with others, especially those who may struggle or need hope. Father, teach me to extend your love to those who differ from me, those who have wronged me, and those who are marginalized in society. May your love be evident in all I say and do, and may it inspire me to be more compassionate, forgiving, and understanding. I pray for this in your holy name. Amen.

Selfless Love

"**G**reater love has no one than this: to lay down one's life for one's friends." John 15:13

I n this verse, Jesus is speaking to his disciples about the ultimate act of love - sacrificing one's life for another. He is teaching them that the greatest expression of love is to lay down one's own life for the sake of another. This selfless act of love puts the needs and well-being of others before one's own. In this teaching, Jesus sets the example of the sacrificial nature of love the disciples should strive to embody in relationships with others.

We may never be required to die for others, but we usually experience the need to sacrifice our time or resources every day. Perhaps you have plans when a friend calls needing a ride. Maybe a family member is in a bad financial situation and needs a loan. Or maybe the need for sacrifice is simply that of your time, to listen to someone and give them encouragement when you would rather do something for yourself. Sacrifice is putting others first. Be like God and love others through your sacrifice.

Today's Prayer

D ear God, throughout the day, help me remember Jesus's example of the ultimate act of love when he laid down his life for me. Help me embody his selfless love in my life. Guide me to seek opportunities to serve others, even when inconvenient or uncomfortable. Give me the strength and courage to put the needs of others before my own and to be willing to make sacrifices. Teach me to love, expecting nothing in return, and to find joy in the act of giving. May my actions and words reflect the selfless love that Jesus expressed, and may I be a constant source of light and hope to those around me. I ask all this in Jesus's name. Amen.

God Loves His Children

"For God so loved the world that he gave his one and only Son, that whoever believes in him shall not perish but have eternal life." John 3:16

This passage illustrates the very depth and extent of God's love for humanity. It shows that God was willing to send his son to die for the sake of humanity's salvation and that his love is available to anyone who believes. God pours out boundless love and grace for his children.

Today's Prayer

Gracious God, I am grateful for the reminder of your deep and abiding love, expressed so powerfully in John 3:16. Help me understand the depth and extent of your love and grow in faith, gratitude, and love. May I be filled with the joy and peace that comes from a personal relationship with you and through trust in you. Thank you for the gift of your son and the hope of eternal life. In his name, I pray. Amen.

God Wants You to Know Him

"Anyone who does not love does not know God, because God is love." 1 John 4:8

Love is an essential aspect of God's nature and character. Anyone who claims to know God but does not show love towards others does not truly know or understand him. Loving others is an important indicator of one's relationship with God. The phrase "to know me is to love me" suggests that if someone gets to know you well, they will come to love you because of your positive qualities, personality, or character. It implies that you are a likable person, and the more people experience your personality, the more they will appreciate and care for you. God already knows and loves you - even if you do not know Him. By getting to know God - through prayer, reading the Bible, and meditating on his qualities and nature - you will deepen your in relationship with the source of all love.

Today's Prayer

Dear God, thank you for your love - pure, unconditional, and eternal. Help me understand you are the source of all love and that I can only genuinely love others when I know and experience your love. Forgive me for the times when I failed to love others and focused on myself instead of extending kindness, compassion, and grace. Teach me to love as you have loved all of us from the beginning and help me seek opportunities to show your love in practical ways. May I always be patient, kind, forgiving, and selfless. May my words and actions reflect your love. I pray for your unending guidance and strength as I seek to love others more deeply and sincerely. I trust you will make me a vessel of your love in this world, which is deeply in need of your light. In Jesus's name, I pray. Amen.

God's Wondrous Works

"Praise the Lord! I will give thanks to the Lord with my whole heart, in the company of the upright, in the congregation. Great are the works of the Lord, studied by all who delight in them. Full of splendor and majesty is his work, and his righteousness endures forever. He has caused his wondrous works to be remembered; the Lord is gracious and merciful. He provides food for those who fear him; he remembers his covenant forever." Psalm 111:1-5

The psalmist expresses his desire to give thanks and praise to the Lord with his whole heart, while among other believers, who are also upright members of the congregation. It is wonderful to praise the Lord and show him adoration and gratitude. God is worthy of all our worship and praise, and our hearts should be filled with thankfulness for all his blessings. Today's scripture reminds us we should cultivate gratitude toward God, and to reflect on all how he has blessed us. Make the conscious effort to give thanks to God with your whole heart - your whole person - and do so in the company of other believers. The act of giving thanks and praise to God should come from our deep inside our spirit, our heart, not just from our lips. And while you praise, try not to let other thoughts or intentions mingle with your feelings about God. Stay focused on him.

The Lord's works in our lives are evidence of His power and wisdom, and they reveal His character and nature to us. His works are things of beauty and grandeur, and they reflect his righteousness and endurance. God's works are not temporary or fleeting, but they last for all time and testify to His greatness. Just observe the beauty and awe of the Grand Canyon, the vast majestic oceans, or the starry night skies and try not to praise God.

Today's Prayer

Dear Lord, I come before you with a grateful heart and give thanks for your great and mighty works. Your creation is full of splendor and majesty, and your righteousness endures forever. We remember and delight in your wondrous works, and your power and glory fill us with awe and respect. Thank you for your graciousness and mercy and for providing for your children. You have never forgotten your covenant with your people, and because of that, I trust in your faithfulness and love. You sent redemption to your people, and you commanded that covenant to last forever. I am grateful for your demonstration of unconditional love and ask you to continue to bless me with your presence, guidance, and provision. Help me always observe the greatness of your works and delight in them. I pray for a heart filled with gratitude and for the ability to reflect your righteousness and love back to those I meet every day. I will praise your name forever and now ask that your blessings always be upon me. I pray this in the name of Jesus Christ, my Lord and Savior. Amen.

More Than Conquerors

"No, in all these things we are more than conquerors through him who loved us." Romans 8:37

This verse emphasizes that believers in Christ can be victorious over the trials and tribulations of life. The phrase "more than conquerors" suggests that the victory won by Christians is not just a narrow, hard-fought win, but a complete and overwhelming triumph. The source of this victory is "him who loved us", Jesus Christ. Through faith in Christ, believers have access to a power and a strength that is beyond what they could achieve on their own. This power comes from God's love, which Apostle Paul believes to be strong enough to overcome any obstacle.

To become more than the conquerors Paul talks about in this verse, we must first accept Jesus as lord and savior in our lives. We do this by acknowledging our need for forgiveness and confessing our sins to him. Once we have entered this new relationship, we must follow Jesus's guidance and grow in our faith through study of the Word, in prayer, and through Christian fellowship.

Today's Prayer

D ear Heavenly Father, as I come before you today, I thank you for your faithfulness and your love. I know that in all things, I am more than a conqueror through your Son, Jesus Christ. Please fill me with your Holy Spirit today and every day, so I can face all the challenges and trials that arise in my life. Help me trust you and rely on your strength, knowing that you are always with me - even when I feel alone and out of solutions. I pray you give me a bold and courageous spirit, so I can conquer my fears. Help me grow in spirit and mature my faith in a way that brings you glory and draws others to you. Thank you for your grace and mercy, and for the victory I have through the sacrifice of your Son. May I walk in His victory today and always. In Jesus's name, I pray. Amen.

God's Masterpiece

"For we are God's masterpiece, created in Christ Jesus to do good works, which God prepared in advance for us to do." Ephesians 2:10

Today's scripture tells us that God did not just create us: we are his beautiful and unique creations - his handiwork. The verse also suggests that God takes great care and attention in creating each of us with a specific purpose in mind for our lives. God calls us to use our lives to make a positive impact on the world. The phrase "created in Christ Jesus" emphasizes that our new life and purpose come from being united with Christ through faith. The phrase "for good works" emphasizes the purpose of not only receiving God's salvation but also actively taking part in virtuous deeds for his glory. God has already prepared these good works for us to do, and he has a specific plan for each of our lives. We can trust him to guide us in carrying out his will.

Today's Prayer

Heavenly Father, thank you for making me a masterpiece. Thank you for designing me with a unique purpose and plan in mind. I am grateful that I am created in Christ Jesus to do good works, and that you have already prepared these good works in advance for me to do. Help me trust in your plan for my life, even when it is difficult or unclear. Give me the strength and wisdom to do the good works you have prepared for me and to make a positive impact on the world around me. Help me remember my identity is in Christ, and I am not defined by past mistakes or current struggles. Help me see myself as you see me - a beloved child created with purpose and intention. Thank you for your unfailing love and grace, which sustain me each day. I pray all of this in Jesus's name. Amen.

Love is the Model

"Love is patient, love is kind. It does not envy, it does not boast, it is not proud. It does not dishonor others, it is not self-seeking, it is not easily angered, it keeps no record of wrongs. Love does not delight in evil but rejoices with the truth. It always protects, always trusts, always hopes, always perseveres." 1 Corinthians 13:4-7

This passage emphasizes the importance of love and says even if someone has great spiritual gifts, knowledge, or faith, without love, those things are meaningless. The passage describes what love is and what it is not, highlighting the characteristics of love, such as patience, kindness, humility, and selflessness. The passage concludes by noting that love is enduring and always protects, trusts, hopes, and perseveres. It is a popular passage for weddings and is often used to encourage people to live a life marked by love.

The New Testament features many with examples of Jesus showing patience, kindness, and humility. For example:

Patience. Jesus showed endless patience dealing with people, even those who were challenging. He often took the time to listen to people's needs and concerns and to teach them principles of love and Godliness through parables and stories. He also showed patience in his interactions with his disciples, who often struggled to understand his teachings.

Kindness. Jesus showed kindness in a variety of ways, such as healing the sick, feeding the hungry, and comforting the grieving. He also showed kindness to the people that his society marginalized or oppressed, such as women, children, and Samaritans. His willingness to help people and show them compassion often characterized Jesus's kindness.

Humility. Jesus showed humility through not only his willingness to die for the sins of all humankind, but also to serve others during his ministry, even those considered lowly or unworthy. He washed his disciples' feet as an example of how they should serve one another, and he often associated with those considered outcasts or sinners. Jesus also showed humility in his willingness to submit to God's will, even to the point of death on the cross.

Overall, Jesus' life and teachings serve as a model of how to live with patience, kindness, and humility, and his example continues to inspire and guide many people today.

Today's Prayer

Heavenly Father, I come before you today and ask for the grace to live a life of love. Help me be patient with others and show kindness in all situations. Keep me from envy and boasting and from being arrogant or rude. Help me put the needs of others before my own and avoid being easily angered or keeping a record of wrongs. May I always delight in the truth and reject evil, protecting others and trusting in your faithfulness. May I always have hope, even in difficult circumstances, and persevere through challenges, knowing that your love never fails. I pray you fill me with your love and enable me to show your love to those around me. May the love of Christ shape my words and guide my actions, and may I be a blessing to all those I encounter. I ask these things in the name of Jesus, who demonstrated perfect love through his life, death, and resurrection. Amen.

Love One Another

"A new commandment I give to you, that you love one another: just as I have loved you, you also are to love one another." John 13:34

Jesus delivers this commandment to his disciples during the Last Supper, where he is preparing them for his imminent death and departure from the natural world. In this verse, Jesus tells the disciples to love one another as he has loved them - selflessly and sacrificially. When we "love one another" like Jesus loves us, we show each other affection, kindness, and compassion. We should show love in our actions, not just in our words, and our love should extend to all people, not just those within our own family, social group, or community. This commandment is often called the "new commandment" because it emphasizes the importance of love as the foundation of the Christian faith and practice.

Today's Prayer

Dear God, thank you for the example of love Jesus showed to me. Help me love others as he loves me, with selfless and sacrificial love. May I be willing to serve and lay down my life for others, just as Jesus did. I pray for the strength and courage to love others, even those who are difficult to love. Help me be patient, kind, and compassionate and help me extend grace and forgiveness to others, as Jesus did for all of us. May my love reflect your love, and may it bring you glory. In Jesus's name, I pray. Amen.

God's Love is Genuine

"Let love be genuine. Abhor what is evil; hold fast to what is good. Love one another with brotherly affection. Outdo one another in showing honor." Romans 12:9-10

This verse admonishes us to cultivate sincere and authentic love for others. We should strongly dislike anything evil or harmful, but cling tightly to things that are beneficial. We should try to love and care for others like we would our own family and always strive to treat others with respect and honor, even going beyond in showing them appreciation and admiration. Many Christians believe that living a life of love, kindness, and respect for others is pleasing to God and can bring fulfillment and purpose to our lives.

Today's Prayer

Dear God, I seek to understand and live out the teachings of your word. Today, I focus on Romans 12:9-10, which instructs believers to let love be genuine, to hate what is evil, and to cling to what is good. Lord, help me put these teachings into practice in my daily life. I ask for the strength to love others with sincerity and authenticity, to stand against evil, and to uphold and amplify good. May brotherly affection and mutual respect shape my relationships with others, and may I always strive to outdo others in showing honor. I pray for your guidance, wisdom, and grace as I seek to do your will. Help me live a life that is pleasing to you and reflects your love and light in the world. I pray this in Jesus's name. Amen.

Praying is Good

" First of all, then, I urge that supplications, prayers, intercessions, and thanksgivings be made for all people, for kings and all who are in high positions, that we may lead a peaceful and quiet life, godly and dignified in every way." 1 Timothy 2:1-2

These verses encourage us to pray for all people, including those in positions of authority, in order to promote peace and godliness in society. This means that as individuals, we should not only pray for ourselves and our loved ones, but also for our leaders and all those who hold positions of power and influence in our society. By praying for our leaders, we express trust in God's sovereignty and acknowledging that he is ultimately in control. We also recognize that those in positions of authority need God's guidance and wisdom to make decisions that will benefit the common good. This passage reminds us we have a responsibility to promote peace and Godliness in our daily lives. We should live in a way that reflects our faith and values, treat others with love and respect, and contribute to the well-being of our communities. This passage reminds us that as individuals, we have a role to play in building a better society, and that our actions and attitudes can have a significant impact on those around us.

Today's Prayer

Dear Heavenly Father, I come before you today with a grateful heart, thanking you for your goodness and mercy. I thank you for the gift of prayer and the privilege of approaching you with my requests. As I read 1 Timothy 2:1-2, I am called to pray for all people, especially for those in positions of authority. I lift up my leaders to you, dear God, asking for your wisdom and guidance upon them. I pray for government officials, community leaders, law enforcement officers, business executives, and all others who are entrusted with leadership roles. May they seek your will in all that they do and make decisions that honor you and benefit society. I also pray for my neighbors, friends, enemies, and everyone in between. May your grace and mercy be upon them, and may they come to know you and experience your love in a deeper way.

Finally, I pray for myself, that I may live in a way that promotes peace and Godliness. Help me love others as you love me, treat others with respect and kindness, and make a positive impact on my family, community, and society. We ask all these things in the name of your Son, Jesus Christ, who taught us to pray, saying, "Our Father in heaven, hallowed be your name. Your kingdom come, your will be done, on earth as it is in heaven. Give us this day our daily bread, and forgive us our debts, as we also have forgiven our debtors. And lead us not into temptation, but deliver us from evil. For yours is the kingdom and the power and the glory forever. Amen."

Peace in Anxious Times

"Do not be anxious about anything, but in everything by prayer and supplication with thanksgiving, let your requests be made known to God. And the peace of God, which surpasses all understanding, will guard your hearts and your minds in Christ Jesus." Philippians 4:6-7

These verses are a reminder for believers not to worry or be anxious about anything, but to bring all concerns and requests to God through prayer and gratitude. By doing so, we can experience the peace of God that goes beyond human understanding, which can protect our hearts and minds. It emphasizes the importance of relying on God's strength and peace rather than our own efforts or worries. This passage is further evidence of God's love for us. By guiding us away from worry and anxiety and instructing us to make our requests known to Him with thanksgiving through prayer, God is explicitly showing that he cares about our well-being and wants us to experience peace in our lives. He promises that if we go to him in prayer, he will give us his peace, unlike any we've experienced in the natural, and it will guard our hearts and minds. God loves us and wants us to be well - physically and mentally!

Today's Prayer

D ear God, I come to you with a grateful heart, thanking you for your goodness and love. I acknowledge you are in control of all things and that I can bring my worries and concerns to you through prayer. I ask that you help me trust in your care and surrender my anxieties to you. I pray for the peace that surpasses all understanding to fill my heart and mind and to guard me in Christ Jesus. I also pray for those facing difficult circumstances or challenging situations. Please give them the strength and courage to persevere and help them experience your peace amid their struggles. Finally, I ask you to continue guiding my life so that I may honor you in all I do. May I be a blessing to those around me and may your love shine through me. I pray this in the name of Jesus Christ, my Lord and Savior. Amen.

Letting Go of Past Mistakes

"Remember your mercy, O LORD, and your steadfast love, for they have been from of old. Remember not the sins of my youth or my transgressions; according to your steadfast love remember me, for the sake of your goodness, O LORD!" Psalm 25:6-7

In this passage, the psalmist pleads with God to remember his mercy and steadfast love, rather than the author's past mistakes. It is a passage of comfort and hope in times of struggle, guilt, or shame, and it encourages us to turn to God about our own shortcomings and ask for forgiveness and grace.

First, the verses highlight the importance of acknowledging our mistakes and taking responsibility for our actions. By asking God to overlook the sins of youth, the author acknowledges past missteps and seeks redemption. Reflect on your own life and take ownership of your actions, rather than ignore or deny them.

Second, the passage reminds us of God's "steadfast," unchanging love and mercy, which are independent of our own merit or worthiness. In this, we have hope that no matter how far we may have strayed or how many mistakes we may have made, we can always turn to God for forgiveness and restoration. The Word instructs us to take responsibility for our actions, seek forgiveness, and trust in God's unfailing love and mercy, which is steadfast, loyal, and true.

Today's Prayer

Dear God, I come before you today with a humble heart, admitting that I have made mistakes and have shortcomings. I ask for your forgiveness and mercy. Please help me let go of the past and not be burdened by my past mistakes. Help me focus instead on your unchanging love and grace, present since time began and available to me now. Guide me to live a life pleasing to you, make amends where necessary, and strive to become a better person each day. I trust in your unfailing love and faithfulness, knowing that you are always with me and will never leave. Thank you for your never-ending compassion and support. In Jesus's name, I pray. Amen.

Finding Comfort in God's Tender Love

"The Lord your God is with you, he is mighty to save. He will take great delight in you, he will quiet you with his love, he will rejoice over you with singing." Zephaniah 3:17

This passage reveals the tender and personal nature of God's love for us. It offers a message of hope and comfort, reassuring us that God is present in our lives and has the desire to love and care for us. The verse says that God is with us, meaning He is present and attentive to our needs. What a source of comfort in times of distress or uncertainty! We also learn that God is "mighty to save," meaning he is powerful and able to rescue us from danger and harm. This reminds us we can trust in God's strength and protection, even when we feel weak or vulnerable. We also learn God takes pleasure in us and desires to soothe our fears and anxieties with his love, like earthly parents. The image of God rejoicing over us in song is powerful, emphasizing the depth of His affection. Imagine God singing - and singing about you! Zephaniah clearly shows us God's love and care can bring great comfort and encouragement in any circumstance. We are never alone: God is always with us, celebrating us.

Today's Prayer

D ear God, as I reflect on the words of Zephaniah 3:17, I am reminded of your soothing love and delight in me. Thank you for your promise to be with me always and for your mighty power to save me from harm. Help me rest in your love and find peace in your presence. May your love quiet me, and may I hear your rejoicing for me. I ask that you help me trust in you and let go of any fears or doubts that may hold me back from fully submitting to your love. Give me the courage to walk in faith, knowing that you are with me every step of the way. Thank you for your faithful love, which endures forever. May I always be mindful of your goodness and grace and seek to share your love with others as you have with me. In Jesus's name, I pray. Amen.

Finding Assurance in His Unfailing Love

"For I am convinced that neither death nor life, neither angels nor demons, neither the present nor the future, nor any powers, neither height nor depth, nor anything else in all creation, will be able to separate us from the love of God that is in Christ Jesus our Lord." Romans 8:38-39

This powerful reminder of the unbreakable and unfailing love that God has for His people offers a message of eternal hope and assurance. It reminds us that no matter what life challenges we face, we can be confident in God's love for us. This includes the past, present, and future. God's omnipresent love saturates every aspect of our lives. The passage emphasizes that nothing in all of creation can separate us from God's love. No obstacle or circumstance can come between us and God's care and affection. This offers great comfort, especially when we struggle with feelings of loneliness or abandonment.

Imagine that you are holding a balloon in your hand. No matter how hard you try to let go of it, the balloon stays attached to your hand. That is how much God's love holds onto you. No matter what you go through, no matter how much you might want to run away, God's love will never let go of you. His love is greater than anything in the world, and nothing can ever separate you from it. Romans 8:38-39 is a powerful statement of God's unwavering love for His people and can be a source of strength and encouragement in any circumstance.

Today's Prayer

D ear God, thank you for your unfailing love, which is greater than anything I can imagine. I am grateful that no matter what I am facing, I can be confident that nothing can separate me from your love. Help me remember this truth in times of doubt or difficulty. Thank you for the hope and assurance that comes from knowing that I am loved. May I be filled with joy and peace, even during life's challenges, knowing that you hold me securely in your love, and may I find strength and courage knowing that you are always with me, and nothing can separate me from your care and protection. I pray you will continue to draw me closer to you and help me live in a way that honors you and brings glory to your name. Thank you for your faithful love, which endures forever. In Jesus' name, I pray. Amen.

Finding Comfort as a Child of God

"See what great love the Father has lavished on us, that we should be called children of God! And that is what we are!" 1 John 3:1

This verse is so powerful. It reminds us that as believers in Jesus Christ, God adopted us into His family and considers us his children. It emphasizes the profound love that God has for us and the incredible privilege it is to be called his sons and daughters. This verse offers a message of hope and assurance, and it reminds us that no matter who we are or what we have done, God welcomes us as part of the family—through faith in Jesus. It also reminds us of the incredible value and worth that we have as children of God, and the immense love and care that our heavenly father has for us. This verse is a beautiful expression of God's love and the incredible gift from God: adoption into his family. Let this passage be a source of comfort, joy, and hope for when you struggle or feel lost. It will remind you of God's unshakable love and support.

Today's Prayer

Heavenly father, thank you for your abiding love and the amazing gift of being adopted as your child. Although I battle a nature susceptible to sin and sometimes act in ungodly ways, you continue to forgive me and still welcome me into your family through your inexhaustible grace and mercy. I am so incredibly grateful for your faithful love and enduring forgiveness. I pray for those who may struggle to understand or accept your love and ask you to help them become your children through faith. May they experience the depth and richness of your love, and may they come to understand their true worth and value as your sons and daughters. May they find hope and comfort knowing that you will never leave or forsake them, and that your love will never fail. I pray that your love fills their hearts and minds, and they will be drawn into a deeper relationship with you. May they know the joy and peace that comes from being in your family, and may they live in a way that honors you and brings glory to your name. I pray all these things in Jesus's name. Amen.

God's Great Love

"The steadfast love of the Lord never ceases; his mercies never come to an end; they are new every morning; great is your faithfulness." Lamentations 3:22-23

The book of Lamentations is a collection of poems that mourn the destruction of Jerusalem and the suffering of the Jewish people. Yet during this despair, we find a glimmer of hope. These verses remind us that even in life's darkest moments, God's love remains steadfast. His mercies never end, and they are new every day. This means we can trust in God's faithfulness and goodness, even when everything around us seems to fall apart. It is easy to get caught up in the difficulties and challenges of life. We may feel like we are drowning in problems with no way out. But Lamentations 3:22-23 reminds us that God's love and mercy are greater than any problem we face. His grace is sufficient for us, and his faithfulness is unchanging. So today, let us remember we serve God, who never gives up on us. His mercies are new every morning, and his love never ceases. May we find hope and comfort in this truth, and may we trust in God's faithfulness as we face the challenges of each day.

Today's Prayer

Dear Lord, thank you for your steadfast love and never-ending mercies. I praise you for your great and eternal faithfulness. I often get caught up in my problems and struggles, forgetting that your love and grace are greater than anything I face. Help me trust you each day with everything, knowing that your mercies are renewed daily. Give me strength to face any challenges that come my way and help me find hope and comfort in your love. May I never forget that you are faithful and will never abandon me. I pray this in Jesus's name. Amen.

Thankful for God's Enduring Love

"Give thanks to the Lord, for he is good. His love endures forever." Psalm 136:1

Psalm 136 is a hymn of thanksgiving, praising God for his mighty works and enduring love. Each verse begins with the refrain, "His love endures forever," reminding us that God's love is constant and unchanging. In the passage, the psalmist invites us to give thanks to the Lord because he is good. We see God's goodness in his creation, his provision, and his salvation. He faithfully keeps his promises, and his love never fails.

This verse reminds us that thankfulness is an essential part of our relationship with God. When we give thanks to the Lord, we acknowledge his goodness and his love for us. We express our gratitude for all that he has done in our lives, and we give him praise for his faithfulness. In giving thanks, we shift our focus from our problems to God's provision, reminding us of his enduring love and filling us with hope and joy! This process of thanksgiving, reflection, and joy strengthens our faith and better enables us to face life's challenges. Give thanks to the Lord today because he is good to us and his love for us never ends. Let your heart overflow with gratitude and never forget to notice God's loving kindness in your life.

Today's Prayer

Dear Lord, thank you for your enduring love and goodness. I praise you for all that you have done in my life and for keeping your promises to your children. Help me cultivate a heart filled with gratitude and to give you thanks each day under all circumstances. May my life be a testimony to your love, and may I never forget that your love lasts forever. In Jesus's name, I pray. Amen.

The Meaning of True Love

"Greater love has no one than this, that someone lay down his life for his friends." John 15:13

This verse powerfully reminds us of the ultimate sacrifice Jesus made for us and challenges us to reflect on what it means to love others. First, we recognize that love is sacrificial. Just as Jesus was willing to sacrifice his life for us, we, too, are called to love others through sacrifice. This may mean giving up our time, resources, or desires for the sake of others. Second, we can recognize that love is selfless. Jesus laid down his life not for his own benefit - but for ours. When we love others, we should do so by expecting nothing in return. We should seek to serve and bless others, not to gain recognition or praise for ourselves. Finally, we recognize that love is relational. Jesus laid down his life for his friends, emphasizing the importance of relationships with others. When we love others, we should seek to build deep, meaningful relationships with them. We should listen, encourage, and support one another, just as Jesus did with his disciples. As we meditate on this verse, may we be inspired to accept sacrifice for love, practice selflessness in love, and seek relationships in love - as Jesus loves us!

Today's Prayer

Father, I thank You for the great love you have for each one of your children. I thank you for the love you showed through the gift of your son Jesus, who showed the greatest love of all in laying down his life for me. As I meditate on this verse, I pray I come to understand the depth of your love and ask you to fill me with a desire to love others as you do, with sacrifice and selflessness. Help me recognize true love is not just a feeling, but an action. May I be willing to put aside my life, interests, and comforts for the sake of others, just as Jesus did. I pray for your love to transform me from the inside out, so that I may love others in a way that brings glory to your name. May your love guide me in all that I do, and may I show your love to others. In Jesus' name, I pray. Amen.

Comfort and Peace in God's Love

"As the Father has loved me, so have I loved you. Abide in my love." John 15:9

Have you ever felt like you are just an ordinary person with nothing particularly special to offer? Maybe you look at other people who seem to have exceptional talents or accomplishments, and you feel you do not measure up. But the good news is, you do not have to possess amazing powers for God to love you or use you.

In John 15:9, Jesus says, "As the Father has loved me, so have I loved you. Abide in my love." This verse reminds us that Jesus's love for us is not based on our achievements or abilities, but on the fact that we are His children. God loves us because he is love. And when we abide in his love, we see ourselves and others differently. We realize that everyone, no matter how ordinary they may seem, has inherent value and worth in God's eyes. We also recognize that our true purpose in life is not to impress others or achieve success, but to love God and love others. Apostle Paul wrote in 1 Corinthians 12:12-27 that each person is a valuable part of the body of Christ, and that every member, no matter how seemingly insignificant, is necessary for the body to function properly.

So, if you are feeling like you are ordinary or unexceptional, remember that God loves and values you! He has a unique purpose and plan for your life and wants to use you to have influence in the world, no matter how ordinary you may feel. Abide in his love and let him transform you from the inside out.

Today's Prayer

Dear God, thank you for the comfort and security I find in you. You are my rock and my refuge, my strength, and my shield. As I come to you now, I ask you to wrap me in your love and bring peace to my heart and mind. I give you all of my worries and fears, knowing that you care for me and that you have everything under control. Help me trust you completely and be at peace in your goodness and faithfulness. Thank you for the blessings you pour into my life and for all the ways you show me love and grace. I am so grateful for your provision and protection and for the many ways that you have sustained me through challenging times. As I go about my day, I pray I reflect your love and kindness to everyone I meet. Help me see others as you see them and to be a source of encouragement and hope wherever I go. In Jesus's name, I pray. Amen.

First, Love

"We love because he first loved us." 1 John 4:19

As Christians, we are called to love one another as God loves us (John 13:34). However, we cannot love others purely out of our own strength or goodness. In fact, John reminds us that our ability to love is rooted in God's love for us. Think about it: before we knew God, before we even existed, God already loved us. He loved us so much that he sent his Son to die for our sins and to reconcile us to him (John 3:16). He loved us so much that he chose us to be his children and heirs (Ephesians 1:5-6). He loves us so much that he continues to pursue us and transform us into his image every day.

When we realize the depth and breadth of God's love, everything changes for us. We no longer have to strive to earn God's love or the love of others. We no longer have to fear rejection or loneliness, because the perfect love of our heavenly father has embraced us. We no longer have to hold grudges or withhold forgiveness, because we have been forgiven and seek to forgive. We no longer have to live only for ourselves, because we God's selfless, sacrificial love encourages to sacrifice for others.

Take a moment to reflect on God's transformational love today and on how it is transforming your life. Receive his love afresh, right now, and let it overflow to all those around us as we go about our day. Remember that we love because he first loved us - and he continues to show how we should love. Thank him for the privilege of being his beloved child.

Today's Prayer

Dear father in heaven, thank you for your perfect love and for loving me first. Thank you for sending your son Jesus to die for my sins and reconcile our relationship. Thank you for choosing me to be your child and heir, and for continuing to transform me into your image day by day. As I reflect on your love today, I am humbled and grateful. I recognize I cannot love others purely out of my strength or goodness, but only through your grace and power, at work in me now. I pray you will fill me with your love today. Help me receive it and let it overflow to others I interact with throughout the day. Help me see others as you do and love them with the same selfless, sacrificial love that you show me. And I pray that your love will be evident in my life, drawing others to you and pointing them to you, the source of all goodness. May that truth of your love continue to transform and shape me into the person you have called me to be. In Jesus's name, I pray. Amen.

God's Love is Steadfast

"But you, O Lord, are a God merciful and gracious, slow to anger and abounding in steadfast love and faithfulness." Psalm 86:15

Have you ever felt like you were on the receiving end of someone's anger or frustration? Maybe you made a mistake, said the wrong thing, or failed to meet someone's expectations, and as a result, you received harsh words or the cold shoulder. It can be painful and discouraging to experience that kind of rejection or judgment. The good news is that God is not like that.

Psalm 86:15 reminds us that when we go to God with our weaknesses and failures, he does not lash out or condemn us. Instead, he shows us mercy and gives us grace. He is patient and kind, never giving up on us or growing tired of our struggles. He is faithful and true, always keeping his promises and working for our good.

In fact, God's love is so steadfast and unwavering that he sent his son to show us how to love each other and to sacrifice himself willingly for the forgiveness of sins (Romans 5:8). Jesus accepted punishment for our sins so we could reconcile with God and experience his mercy and grace forever - if we believe in Jesus's sacrifice and resurrection. And even now, as we continue to stumble and fall, Jesus intercedes for us, for forgiveness and restoration (Hebrews 7:25). So, if you are feeling weighed down by your mistakes or discouraged by your failures, take heart. Our God is merciful and gracious, slow to anger, and steadfast in his love and faithfulness. He sees you, knows you, and loves you. He invites you to come to him with confidence, knowing that he will welcome you with open arms and forgive you.

"Let us then draw near to God with a sincere heart and with the full assurance that faith brings, having our hearts sprinkled to cleanse us from a guilty conscience and having our bodies washed with pure water." (Hebrews 10:22).

Today's Prayer

Dear father in heaven, thank you for your unwavering love and faithfulness. Thank you for being merciful and gracious. Thank you for being slow to anger and never ceasing in your love. Thank you for sending your Son Jesus to show your love to me in a tangible way. I confess I am not always faithful or loving toward you. I make mistakes, sin, and fall short of your glory. I am so thankful that you never give up on me. You are patient, even when I am slow to learn and quick to forget. You are gracious, even when I do not deserve it. And you are merciful, even when I deserve punishment. Father, I ask for you to help me reflect your character in my life. Help me be merciful and gracious to others, just as you are. Help me be slow to anger and quick to forgive, just as you are. And help me love others with the same steadfast love that you show me. I pray for those who are hurting or struggling today. May they experience your mercy and grace in the natural so that they may believe and draw closer to you, the source of all love and goodness. I thank you for your faithfulness and a love that never fails. May I rest in the assurance of your goodness and trust in your unfailing love. In Jesus's name, I pray. Amen.

God's Love Revealed

"But God demonstrates his own love for us in this: While we were still sinners, Christ died for us." Romans 5:8

God's love is often described as "sacrificial," but what does this characterization really mean? Romans 5:8 gives us a glimpse into the depths of God's love by showing us what it looks like in action. It tells us that God showed his love for us by sending Jesus to die for our past and future sins while we were still sinning.

Think about that for a moment. God did not wait for us to clean up our act or prove our worthiness before He showed us the greatest demonstration of love. He loved us while we were still in our brokenness, selfishness, and ignorance. He loved us even when we were his enemies. He loved us so much that he sent his son to take on punishment and physical death, so that we could start fresh in our relationship with him, with clean hearts and souls.

God sent Jesus to accept the ultimate sacrifice willingly on our behalf. He gave up the most valuable thing - his life - for the sake of others. For us. God sacrificed his son to save us from sin, death, and eternal separation from him, and so we could experience his love and grace. So, what does this mean for us today? We do not have to earn God's love or try to be good enough for him. His love is a gift freely given, and it is available to us no matter what we have done or who we are. Be assured that God loves and accepts us, just as we are.

This also means that we are called to love others in the same sacrificial way that God loves us. We are called to love even when it's hard, to love even those who have hurt us, and to love without condition or expectation of something in return. Let us thank God for his sacrificial love and ask him to help us love others in the same way. May we be reminded that his love is not based on our performance or worthiness but on His gracious and merciful nature. And may we live out that love in our daily lives, bringing hope and healing to a broken world.

Today's Prayer

Heavenly father, I come before you today to thank you for the incredible sacrifice of your Son Jesus who died for us while we were yet sinners. Thank you for demonstrating your love in such a powerful way. Lord, I know that your love is not something I can earn because you freely give it to me. Help me fully receive and embrace your love, and let it transform me to be more like you. I also ask for help with extending the same sacrificial love to others, just as you showed us. Give me the strength and courage to love even those who are difficult and to show compassion and kindness to those in need. Lord, I am not perfect, and I fall short of your glory. But I also know your love covers all my sins and shortcomings. I ask you to continue pouring out your grace and mercy on me, and to guide and empower me to live according to your will. Thank you, Lord, for your love that knows no boundary. May I always be grateful for this love, and may it motivate me to live a life that honors and glorifies you. I ask all these things in the precious name of your son, Jesus Christ. Amen.

Rooted and Grounded in God's Love

" ...So that Christ may dwell in your hearts through faith—that you, being rooted and grounded in love, may have strength to comprehend with all the saints what is the breadth and length and height and depth, and to know the love of Christ that surpasses knowledge, that you may be filled with all the fullness of God." Ephesians 3:17-19

Have you ever experienced the love of Christ - the love that surpasses all understanding and fills you with all the joy and completeness of God? That is the love God gives us. He wants us to be rooted and grounded in his love so that we can experience his love in its fullness. In today's scripture, Paul encourages us to allow Christ to dwell in our hearts through faith, so that we can root and ground ourselves in his love and then develop the ability to comprehend the depth and breadth of God's love, which transcends our natural knowledge and experience.

As we meditate on this passage, think about God's love for us. We can ask Him to help us understand and experience it in all its fullness - all aspects and manifestations of it. We can pray for the strength to remain rooted and grounded in his love, no matter which circumstances we face. May today's prayer encourage you to become rooted and grounded in God's love and may you continue to seek his will and his way in all that you do.

Today's Prayer

D ear heavenly father, thank you for the boundless love that surpasses all understanding. Help me become rooted and grounded in your love, so that I may truly experience its fullness. Give me the strength and will to seek Christ's love and be filled with your joy. May I remain steadfast in faith, no matter what challenges I encounter. Help me remember your love never fails, and I can always rely on it. Please continue to guide and lead me on the path you set for me. May I always seek your will and your way, and may your love be the foundation of everything I do. In Jesus's name, I pray. Amen.

Godly Characteristics

"The Lord is merciful and gracious, slow to anger and abounding in steadfast love." Psalm 103:8

Negativity, conflict, and chaos bombard us, coming at us from all directions: family, friends, work, news media, politicians, social media, etc. It is easy to get caught up in the stress and rush of daily life and lose sight of what truly matters. As Christians, we are called to cultivate godly characteristics in our lives, and just as God is merciful, slow to anger, and abounding in steadfast love, be more like him.

To be merciful and gracious means to show kindness and compassion to others, even when we think they do not deserve it. This is a challenge, especially when they hit us with negativity, drama, and strife. We are often quick to judge and criticize, but if we reflect on the mercy and grace God extends to us, we can learn to extend the same kindness and compassion to others, no matter how much chaos they bring with them.

To be slow to anger means to be patient and level-headed in the face of adversity. This is an essential characteristic to cultivate and counteract the likelihood of being easily triggered, insulted, offended, or irritated. By practicing patience and self-control, we avoid unnecessary conflicts and misunderstandings in our personal and professional lives. Being slow to anger is being godly.

To be abounding in steadfast love means to love others unconditionally and without fail. Godly love is sacrificial and selfless, and it transforms lives. By loving others with the same love God shows us, we will make a positive impact on the world and transcend it. Abounding in steadfast love is practicing godliness.

Finally, to trust in God means to put our faith and hope in Him, even amid life's challenges. When we trust God, he will guide us and sustain us through all situations. God's steadfastness and eternal love for us provides the secret weapon against the enemy's best attempts to make us lose our cool through the chaos, negativity, and strife. Trusting in God means trusting in love and its power to soothe, protect, and heal. Let us cultivate these godly characteristics, and amid the chaos of the natural world, become the light of God's love in a shadowy world. By so doing, we can be the experience of God for others.

Today's Prayer

Dear God, thank you for the characteristics highlighted in Psalm 103:8. I am grateful for your mercy, grace, delayed anger, and steadfast love. Help me cultivate these same characteristics in my life, so I can reflect your love and grace to others. May I always be merciful and gracious toward others, even when I think they do not deserve it. Help me be patient and calm in the face of adversity. May I love others with the love that you show me, one that is sacrificial and selfless. And may I always trust in you, especially amid life's challenges, when I might be tempted to give up on your faithfulness. I pray you let your light shine through me in this murky world, and that I will reflect your love and grace to everyone I encounter. May your name be glorified in all I do. In Jesus' name, I pray. Amen.

Living in God's Love

"And so, we know and rely on the love God has for us. God is love. Whoever lives in love lives in God, and God in them." 1 John 4:16

God's love is something we can rely on and trust in every single day of our lives. We know God loves us because he took human form as Jesus Christ and willingly died as a sacrifice for our sins. This selfless act of love shows the depth of God's feelings for us and the lengths that he will go to show that love.

1 John 4:16 reminds us that God is love. This means that every aspect of God's being is filled with love. His thoughts, actions, and intentions are all driven by his love for us. When we live in love, we are living in God and being godly because we are showing his love for others. To be godly, which means to be loving, we show compassion, forgiveness, and kindness to others, just as God shows these qualities to us. Loving others means we put their needs above our own and look out for their well-being. We are called to love our neighbors as ourselves, and this is only possible when we are living in God's love. Living in God's love also means that we are allowing Him to live in us. When we live in love, we are inviting God's Spirit to dwell within us and transform us into the people He wants us to be. God's love is powerful, and it can change us from the inside out. Take time today to reflect on

God's love and how you can live in and show that love. Ask God to help us show God-level love to those around us and open our hearts to his transformative power. When we live in God's love, we are living in the God's presence. There is no greater place to be.

Today's Prayer

Dear Lord, thank you for the message of your unfailing love, so clearly expressed in today's verse. Help me hold on to this truth in my heart and live my life as a reflection of your love. I humbly ask for your blessing and for help to walk in the light of your love each day. May I be reminded of Your love when facing challenges, and may I find strength and hope in Your love in all circumstances. I pray you help me love others with the same selfless love you show me and that your love is a light that shines through me and draws others to you. Thank you, Lord, for your love that never fails. May we always trust in your love and live our lives in a way that brings honor and glory to you. May your word continue to speak to my heart and transform me into the likeness of Jesus. In his name, I pray. Amen.

Unshakable Love

" For the mountains may depart and the hills be removed, but my steadfast love shall not depart from you, and my covenant of peace shall not be removed, says the Lord, who has compassion on you." Isaiah 54:10

Life can be unpredictable and full of unexpected challenges. In moments of uncertainty and fear, it is easy to feel insecure and unsteady. But as believers, we have a firm foundation in the unshakable love of God. Isaiah 54:10 reminds us that even if the mountains were to depart and the hills be removed, God's love for us will remain steadfast and unwavering.

What does it mean to have an unshakable love? It means that God's love for us is not based on external conditions, our circumstances, or our actions. His love is not conditional or fleeting. God's love is constant, never changing, and always available. We can trust in his love to be our anchor during life's storms. God's unshakable love also means that we have security in our relationship with him. We should not fear that he will leave or abandon us. He has made a covenant of peace with us, through Jesus' sacrifice, and that is eternal - it cannot be withdrawn. This covenant is a promise of his presence and commitment to care for us.

When we rest in God's unshakable love, we can find peace and security in the middle of chaos. We can trust he is with us, no matter what we face, what we do, and what happens to us. We can also share his unconditional, everlasting love with others, knowing that it is an unfailing, forever love. Take time today to reflect on God's unshakable love for you. Thank him for his faithfulness and for his commitment to be with you at all times. Ask him to help you trust in his love and to share it with others. Remember that no matter what happens, his love for you will never change.

Today's Prayer

Dear God, I come before you today with a grateful heart and thanks for your unshakable love. I know that in this ever-changing world, your love is the one thing that remains constant and unwavering. I am so thankful that your covenant of peace brings me security and comfort. Lord, I pray for the ability to trust in your love more fully. Help me remember that even when things seem uncertain or difficult, you are with me, holding me, and guiding me. I pray I will find rest in your unshakable love and share it with others. I also lift those who are struggling today, Father. May they feel the embrace of your love and the peace that comes from knowing you. I pray you will provide for their needs and give them strength and courage to face whatever lies ahead. Thank you, God, for your unshakable love that never fails. I ask all these things in Jesus' name. Amen.

Thanks Be to God

" Give thanks to the God of heaven, for his steadfast love endures forever." Psalm 136:26

When you read Psalm 136, you see a beautiful pattern emerge. The psalmist repeats the phrase "his steadfast love endures forever" after each description of God's wondrous deeds. This repetition emphasizes God's enduring love as the underlying motivation for his actions on behalf of his people. The psalm's last verse, 136:26, summarizes the intent and invites us to respond with gratitude to God, who has shown us his steadfast love in so many ways. What does it mean to give thanks to the "God of heaven"? It means to acknowledge him as the source of all good things, to express our gratitude for his blessings, and to honor him as the one who sustains us in all circumstances. It also means to recognize his love as the unchanging foundation of our lives, the bedrock upon which we can build our faith and maintain our hope.

When we give thanks to God for his steadfast love, we acknowledge the truth that he is God who loves us with an everlasting love. We recognize that his love is not fickle or conditional but is solid and unwavering. We are also affirming our own need for his love and our dependence on him for every good thing. As you reflect on today's scripture, give thanks to God for his unwavering and supportive love. Let the Holy Spirit fill your heart with gratitude for all the ways God has shown you, his love. Think about those ways and reflect on their constancy: the kind word a neighbor had for you, the recognition you received at work, or the short line at the grocery store. Each little good thing - as well as the big things - are demonstrations of God's unfailing love. Let his love be the rock upon which you build your life, faith, and hope.

Today's Prayer

Dear God, thank you for the steadfast love that endures forever. Thank you for the many blessings you have given me and the ways you provide for my needs. Help me to always remember that your love is not based on my worthiness or performance, but solely on your will and loving kindness for me. May I remember to honor and praise you every day for your unchanging character and for the gift of your love. In Jesus's name, I pray. Amen.

Finding Satisfaction in God's Love

"Because your steadfast love is better than life, my lips will praise you." Psalm 63:3

Read all of Psalm 63, and tune-in to the psalmist's heart's deep longing for God. He expresses thirst for God's presence and a desire to see God's power and glory. During his trials and difficulties, he clings to God as his refuge and strength. In the third verse, the psalmist proclaims that God's enduring and always-present love is better than his own life. What a powerful declaration of the psalmist's faith and devotion! He will risk everything to be in a relationship with God and to praise and honor him.

"God's steadfast love is better than life" means that we should recognize the ultimate source of joy and fulfillment is in God's love. The verse encourages us to acknowledge that nothing in this world can satisfy the deep longing of our hearts like God's love. It instructs us to affirm that God's love is the foundation of our faith and the reason for our hope.

When we praise God for his steadfast love, we declare him worthy of our deepest gratitude and honor. We express our own love for him and thankfulness for the innumerable ways he shows his love and grace in every moment of our lives. We also acknowledge our need for his love and our dependence on him for everything.

As you reflect on this scripture, embrace the psalmist's declaration. Get this deep down in your spirit: God's steadfast love is better than this life. It is eternal and complete. Let your heart fill with the joy and peace that come from feeling God's love activate in your soul. Open your mouth and praise him for his goodness and mercy. And let his love be the unfailing anchor that holds you steady and secure in the tumultuous storms of life.

Today's Prayer

Dear Heavenly Father, thank you for your steadfast love, a love that is better than life. Nothing in this world can satisfy the longing of my heart like your love. Help me trust in your love and to find joy and peace in your presence. I ask that you open my heart and mind to be receptive to your love and to be transformed by it. May my mouth be filled with praise and thanksgiving for all that you have done for me. I ask for your protection and guidance and for your help in my efforts to walk in your ways and be faithful to you in everything I do. I pray these things in the name of Jesus Christ, who showed that your love is greater than life, which he sacrificed for me. Amen.

Clothing Ourselves with Compassion, Kindness, and Forgiveness

"Therefore, as God's chosen people, holy and dearly loved, clothe yourselves with compassion, kindness, humility, gentleness and patience. Bear with each other and forgive one another if any of you has a grievance against someone. Forgive as the Lord forgave you." Colossians 3:12-13 (ESV)

In Colossians 3:12-13, we see a call to action for believers to adopt qualities that reflect the character of God. To purposefully cover and protect themselves with these qualities as they would with clothing. God instructs us, his chosen people, to cover ourselves with the qualities of compassion, kindness, humility, gentleness, and patience. These are not just suggestions, but commands we must obey if we are to honor God.

Compassion is the ability to feel empathy and sympathy for those who are suffering. As followers of Christ, we are called to be compassionate towards others, just as Jesus is compassionate. Kindness is the act of being generous and helpful to others without expecting anything in return. We are to be kind to one another, especially to those who we deem undeserving. Humility means being modest, courteous, and respectful - not boastful and arrogant. Humility also means putting others before ourselves. Humble people recognize they are not the center of the universe and that they need others' help.

Gentleness is the quality of being kindly, amiable, and not forceful, rough, or violent. God's word tells us to be gentle with one another, especially when dealing with demanding situations or people. Patience enables us to maintain calm in adversity. We must be patient with one another, especially when we deal with stress, change, and volatility. Bearing with one another means being tolerant of each other. It means recognizing that we all have flaws and make mistakes. Forgiveness means letting go of a grievance or pardoning someone for an offense made against you. We are called to forgive others just as Christ forgave us. We should not hold on to grudges or bitterness if we want to live in a manner that honors God.

We are called to "clothe" ourselves with these virtues so that we can reflect God's character. Jesus showed us how to apply these qualities in our daily lives by his example of compassion, kindness, humility, gentleness, patience, bearing with one another, and forgiving one another. To apply these virtues in our lives, we should commit these to memory and intentionally seek to embody them in relationships with others, recognizing that we need God's grace to do so. By following Jesus' example and relying on God's grace, we can live a life that honors God and reflects his character of love and forgiveness.

Today's Prayer

Dear God, as I reflect on your Word, I am reminded of the qualities that you instruct me to cultivate and share every day. Please help me clothe myself with compassion, kindness, humility, gentleness, and patience. I pray these qualities become evident in my life as I interact with others. I also ask for your help in bearing with and forgiving others. I recognize that this is not always easy, but I know with your help, all things are possible. Help me let go of grudges and bitterness and extend forgiveness to those who have wronged me.

GOD'S LOVE IS FOREVER

Thank you for your transformative love and for the forgiveness that you extended through Christ's sacrifice on my behalf. Help me extend that same love and forgiveness to those others. May my life reflect your character and bring you honor and glory. In Jesus's name, I pray. Amen.

Reflecting on the Beatitudes

Have you wanted to do a deeper study of the Beatitudes? These blessings are the foundation of Jesus's teaching, and he delivered them early in his ministry. Refer to the book of Matthew's fifth chapter, verses 5-11 for the full scripture.

The First Beatitude

Surrender

"Blessed are the poor in spirit, for theirs is the kingdom of heaven." Matthew 5:3 (ESV)

Matthew 5 reveals Jesus's teaching on what Christians call The Beatitudes, a collection of blessings for qualities and behaviors God desires us to have and practice. In the first Beatitude, being poor in spirit means to recognize our own spiritual poverty, to acknowledge that we are not self-sufficient and need God's help and guidance in our lives. It means to come to God with a humble and contrite heart, recognizing our own sinfulness and our need for His grace and mercy. In today's culture, society often associates being poor in spirit with weakness and tells us to be self-reliant, pull ourselves up by our own bootstraps, and rely on our own strength and abilities. But Jesus teaches us something quite different: true strength comes from acknowledging our weakness and turning to him for help.

By accepting our spiritual poverty, we recognize that we alone cannot save ourselves from the separation from God caused by our sinful nature and that we need God to save us from it. Surrendering ourselves to God, trusting him, and allowing Him to work in our lives will transform us from the inside out. Surrender requires trust in his provision, his protection, and his guidance.

Surrender and submission to God enable us to experience the kingdom of heaven (God's spirit) in our lives. We find peace, joy, and fulfillment in knowing our heavenly Father loves and cares for us. We experience the blessings our Father gives his children, gifts from his spiritual kingdom, which are not of this world but are eternal and supernatural.

Remember that being poor in spirit is not just about recognizing your need for the Savior. It also recognizes your need for others. When you are poor in spirit, you realize you cannot make it through this life on your own and that you need the support and love from others. As Christians, we reach out to others in humility, ask for help when needed, and offer help when others need it, too.

Applying the Scripture

Try to cultivate a spirit of humility. To apply Matthew 5:3 practically, we can intentionally cultivate a spirit of humility in our daily lives. This could involve things like practicing gratitude for what we have, acknowledging our limitations and weaknesses, and seeking to learn from others who have different perspectives or experiences. It could also involve intentionally seeking opportunities to serve others, such as volunteering at a local charity or helping a neighbor in need.

Prioritize your relationship with God. Another way to apply Matthew 5:3 is to prioritize our relationship with God more than anything else. This could involve making time each day to pray, meditating on scripture, and seeking God's guidance and wisdom. We could also be intentional about attending church or other faith-based gatherings, and seeking relationships with other believers who can encourage and support us in our faith. By prioritizing a relationship with God, we can become more aware of our spiritual poverty and our need for his grace and guidance in our lives.

Let us humble ourselves before God today and ask him to help us be poor in spirit. Let us surrender ourselves to him and trust in his provision and guidance. For in doing so, as Jesus tells us, we will experience the true blessings of the kingdom of heaven.

Today's Prayer

Heavenly Father, I come before you with a humble and contrite heart, recognizing my own spiritual poverty and need for your grace and mercy. I thank you for the blessings of your kingdom, which are available to me when I trust in you and surrender to your will. Help me become poor in spirit, to acknowledge my dependence on you, and to seek your help and guidance in all things. Grant me humility to recognize my own sinful nature and need for forgiveness and grace and give me the courage to confess my sins and seek your mercy. I also pray that you help me be a blessing to others. Show me how to serve those in need, offer help and support to those around me, and be a light in this world. Thank you for the promise that the kingdom of heaven belongs to the poor in spirit. May I experience the blessings of your kingdom in my life today and always. In Jesus's name, I pray. Amen.

The Second Beatitude

Comfort in Times of Sorrow

"Blessed are those who mourn, for they shall be comforted."
Matthew 5:4 (ESV)

Life is full of trials, and in those down times, we may experience depression, sadness, grief, and loss. During difficult periods, we may find it difficult - even impossible - to find any comfort. But God promises us hope and healing, even for those not familiar with the Word. In the Matthew 5 through the Beatitudes, Jesus taught his followers the values and attitudes leading to true happiness and fulfillment. Today's scripture suggests that those who are experiencing grief and sorrow can ultimately find comfort and solace in God.

When we are feeling down or overwhelmed, it is easy to turn inward and focus on our own pain. However, it is important to remember that we are not alone. We have not only the Father, Son, and Holy Spirit for comfort, but also a community of brothers and sisters in Christ who care about us and want to support us. It is also important to turn to God during times of hardship and grief, even if we know little about Scripture. God is always there for us, and He promises comfort and healing.

Applying the Scripture

M atthew 5:4 (ESV) says, "Blessed are those who mourn, for they shall be comforted." Here are two ways to apply this verse in our lives:

Seek comfort in God: When we experience grief, loss, or any form of sorrow, turn to God for comfort. Tell him about your pain and struggle. Ask him for his peace and support. Pray, read the Bible, and seek the support of our faith communities. Trust in God's love and grace, we will find the healing we need.

Show compassion to others. As followers of Jesus, we are called to show compassion to those who are mourning or experiencing sorrow. We can reach out to others with a listening ear, a kind word, or a simple act of service. By showing empathy and love to those around us, we can help to ease their burden and offer comfort in their time of need. Overall, applying Matthew 5:4 in our lives means trusting in God's promise of comfort and healing and extending that same comfort and compassion to those around us.

Today's Prayer

D ear God, I come to you today seeking comfort and solace during this challenging time. I may not know much about Scripture, but I know you are always present and supporting me, and that you promise comfort and healing. Please help me find peace in your love and grace, and to reach out to those who care about me for support and encouragement. In Jesus's name, I pray. Amen.

The Third Beatitude

Humility and Blessings

"**B**lessed are the meek, for they shall inherit the earth." Matthew 5:5 (ESV)

Dear friend, if you are struggling to understand these words, know that Christ is with you always and will guide you as you seek to know him better. The words may seem confusing at first, but I assure you they carry great wisdom and hope! To be meek is not to be weak or powerless, but it means to have your strength under control, not unbridled. Meekness means to have a gentle and humble spirit, to be patient and kind, and to seek peace more than anything else.

In a world that often values strength, power, and aggression, it may seem counterintuitive to embrace meekness and that the meek will triumph. Jesus is telling us that those who cultivate humility, kindness, and a gentle spirit in their lives will ultimately be the ones who truly prosper. They will find joy and contentment in their lives, and they will be blessed with the love and respect of those around them. So do not be afraid to embrace meekness. It is a powerful and beautiful way to live. Trust in Christ's teachings, they will guide you on the path to true happiness and fulfillment.

Applying the Scripture

The following are two examples of how the principle of "Blessed are the meek, for they shall inherit the earth" might play out in practical situations:

1. A coworker is consistently rude and difficult to work with. A meek person responds with kindness and patience, seeking to understand the root of their coworker's behavior and showing them compassion despite their negative attitude. Over time, the meekness leads to a transformation in the coworker's behavior and a more harmonious work environment for all.

2. A person is experiencing financial difficulties and is feeling frustrated and helpless. A meek person responds with humility and a willingness to seek help and support from others. Rather than becoming angry or aggressive, they seek guidance from a financial adviser and reach out to family and friends for help. Through their meekness and willingness to accept help, they ultimately find financial stability and security.

In both examples, meekness leads to positive outcomes and blessings, even in challenging situations. By choosing to respond with kindness, patience, and humility, we can inherit the blessings of the earth and experience greater happiness and fulfillment in our lives.

Today's Prayer

Dear Heavenly Father, we come before you today with hearts open and seeking to understand your teachings more deeply. We know your words are filled with wisdom and truth, but we also acknowledge that we are limited in our understanding. We ask that you help us grasp the meaning behind Christ's words in Matthew 5:5. We pray you guide us to live with a spirit of meekness, choosing kindness and humility even in demanding situations. Help us trust in your plan for our lives and to find joy and contentment in the blessings of the earth. May we experience the love and respect of those around us as we seek to live obediently, according to your instruction. We thank you for your constant presence in our lives and for the gift of Christ, who teaches us how to live with love, grace, and humility. We ask for your continued guidance and blessings as we strive to understand and apply these teachings to our lives. In Jesus' name, we pray. Amen.

The Fourth Beatitude

Satisfaction in Righteousness

"B lessed are those who hunger and thirst for righteousness, for they shall be satisfied." Matthew 5:6 (ESV)

D ear friend, In Matthew 5:6, Christ speaks about hungering and thirsting for righteousness. He tells us that those who seek righteousness with a pure heart will be satisfied. To hunger and thirst for righteousness means to have a fervent desire to do what is right and to live a life that is pleasing to God. It means seeking justice, showing mercy, and walking humbly with our Creator. This hunger and thirst for righteousness can sometimes feel like a burden, especially in a world that often values power, wealth, and success over righteousness. However, Christ assures us that those who hunger and thirst for righteousness will be satisfied. This means that they will find true fulfillment and joy in their lives, and they will experience the blessings of living a righteous life.

Applying the Scripture

To apply this teaching to our lives, we must strive to live with integrity and to seek righteousness in all that we do. We must be honest, kind, and compassionate, showing love and mercy to those around us. We must also be willing to stand up for what is right, even when it is difficult or unpopular.

As we hunger and thirst for righteousness, we can trust in Christ to satisfy us with his love, his grace, and his blessings. He will guide us on the path to righteousness, and we will experience the joy and fulfillment that comes from living a life that is pleasing to God. May we always hunger and thirst for righteousness, knowing that Christ is with us and will satisfy our deepest longings.

Today's Prayer

Dear God, thank you for your teachings about righteousness and for the assurance that those who hunger and thirst for righteousness will be satisfied. Help us develop a powerful desire for what is right and to live our lives with integrity and honor. We pray you guide us on the path to righteousness and that you give us the courage to stand up for what is right, even when it is difficult. May we always show love and compassion to those around us and seek justice and mercy in all that we do. As we strive to live a righteous life, we ask that you satisfy our deepest longings with your love and grace. May we find joy and fulfillment in knowing you and in doing your will. Thank you for your constant presence in our lives and for the gift of your Son, who teaches us how to live with righteousness and grace. We pray all of this in Jesus's name. Amen.

The Fifth Beatitude

The Beauty of Mercy

"**B**lessed are the merciful, for they shall obtain mercy." Matthew 5:7 (ESV)

This scripture speaks to the value of forgiveness and compassion. Those who are merciful towards others will receive mercy and compassion from God. Matthew 5.7 teaches us that being merciful towards others is an essential aspect of living a blessed life. Showing mercy means extending compassion, kindness, and forgiveness to those who have wronged us or who are in need.

In simplest terms, the verse says that if we show mercy to others, we will receive mercy in return. This is not only important in our relationships with others, but also in our relationship with God. We all need God's mercy, and when we show mercy to others, we reflect God's character and love for us. Through acts of mercy, we can experience the fullness of God's love and also receive his mercy. This verse is a reminder that showing mercy to others is not only a good thing to do, but it is also a way to experience the blessings of God in our own lives. Let us strive to be merciful to others, as God has been merciful to us.

Applying the Scripture

It reminds us to treat others the way we would like to be treated. When we show mercy to others, we create a culture of kindness, forgiveness, and love that can uplift our relationships and improve the lives of those around us. It also encourages us to extend grace to ourselves. We are all flawed human beings who make mistakes, and it is important to remember that we, too, need mercy from others and from God. By extending mercy to ourselves, we can learn to forgive ourselves for our shortcomings and move forward with a sense of peace and self-acceptance.

Today's Prayer

Dear Heavenly Father, Matthew 5:7 reminds us that showing mercy to others is important. Mercy helps us to be compassionate, kind, and forgiving towards those who have wronged us or who are in need. May our acts of mercy reflect your character and your love for us. We pray that you also extend your mercy to us, for we are all in need of your grace and forgiveness. Help us extend mercy to ourselves as well, so that we may find peace and self-acceptance despite our flaws and imperfections. We ask for your guidance and strength as we seek to live a blessed life by showing mercy to others. May our actions and words reflect your love and mercy towards us. In Jesus' name, we pray. Amen.

The Sixth Beatitude

Seeing God Through a Purified Heart

"Blessed are the pure in heart, for they shall see God." Matthew 5:8 (ESV)

In this verse, Jesus teaches about having a pure heart. A pure heart is free from sinful desires, motives, and thoughts. It is a heart that seeks to honor God in all things and focuses on Him alone. The promise that the pure in heart shall see God is powerful. It reminds us that God desires to reveal Himself to us, not remain hidden or unattainable, but we must come to him with a heart free from sin. When we seek purification through confession, repentance, and honesty with God, we open ourselves up to experiencing his presence and seeing his work in our lives.

Applying the Scripture

Take some time today to get quiet - away from the noise, your computer, your phone, and other distractions - and examine your heart. Ask God to reveal any areas of sin or impurity. Think about behaviors, beliefs, actions, or ideas that are not Godly and ask God for his forgiveness for those. Ask him to remove them from your spirit and create in you a clean heart. As you seek purification and draw closer to him, ask to experience the blessing of seeing him at work in your life and in the world around you.

Today's Prayer

D ear God, we thank you for the powerful words of Jesus in Matthew 5:8, reminding us of the importance of having a pure heart. Help us examine our hearts and to confess and repent of any sin or impurity that may be hindering our relationship with you. Fill us with your Holy Spirit and empower us to live lives that are pleasing to you. May we experience the blessings of seeing you at work in our lives and in the world. We pray this in Jesus's name. Amen.

The Seventh Beatitude

Reflecting God's Love and Bringing Blessing to Others

"Blessed are the peacemakers, for they shall be called sons of God." Matthew 5:9 (ESV)

The Aramaic word Jesus would have used for "peacemakers" in the original text of the Bible is "'ibnay shlama" (אבני שלמא). This term means "builders of peace" or "sons of peace." Aramaic is the ancient semitic language Jesus and the first writers of the Bible spoke. This verse is a powerful statement from Jesus. In it, he teaches us that when we work to make peace with others, we are doing something that God values - so much that He considers the peacemakers his children.

Being a peacemaker means we seek to resolve conflicts and bring people together, instead of fighting or arguing. This can be difficult, but it is an important part of following Jesus and living in a way that honors God. When we make peace, we reflect God's character and love. God is a peacemaker, and He desires for us to live in harmony with others. When we work to make peace, we become more like God, and also show our love for Him. As we try to be peacemakers, we will probably face challenges and opposition. But we can take heart knowing that God is with us, and He will bless us for our efforts. When we make peace, we show the world that we are children of God, and we bring glory to His name.

Applying the Scripture

Let us strive to be peacemakers in our homes, communities, and the world. Here are two situations in which being a peacemaker had a much better and Godly outcome:

1. The Story of Joseph: In the Bible, Joseph's brothers sold him into slavery, and he ended up in Egypt. Through a series of events, he rose to an elevated position in Pharaoh's court. Years later, when famine struck, Joseph's brothers came to Egypt to buy food, not knowing that they would encounter their long-lost brother whom they wronged. Rather than seeking revenge, Joseph forgave his brothers and welcomed them with open arms. He used his power and position to provide for them and reconcile with them, instead of holding a grudge and seeking retribution. By doing so, Joseph showed the power of forgiveness and reconciliation.

2. The Christmas Truce of 1914: During World War I, on Christmas Day in 1914, soldiers on both sides of the trenches in Europe spontaneously laid down their arms and declared a temporary truce. They sang carols, exchanged gifts, and played football together. This remarkable display of peace and goodwill among enemies showed that even during war, it is possible to find common ground and build bridges between opposing sides. The truce was short-lived, but it provided a brief respite from the horrors of war and a reminder of our shared humanity.

In both examples, being a peacemaker led to positive outcomes that brought people together rather than driving them apart. It allowed for forgiveness, reconciliation, and a recognition of our shared humanity. Let us seek to bring people together and to live in harmony with one another. In doing so, we will honor God, and we will experience the blessings that come from being His children.

Today's Prayer

Dear God, we come before you today with heavy hearts, burdened by the difficulties and challenges of life. We lift up all those who work as peacemakers; those who try to make ends meet, who are struggling to provide for their families, and who are facing seemingly insurmountable obstacles. We pray you give them strength and courage to face each day with hope and perseverance. May they find comfort and peace in knowing that you are with them always, guiding them through the difficulties of life. We ask that you provide for their needs and give them the resources and opportunities they need to thrive. May they find favor in the eyes of others, and may their hard work be rewarded with success and prosperity. Most of all, we pray you fill them with your love and grace. May they feel your presence in their lives, and may they find hope and peace amid their struggles. We thank you for the gift of work and for the ability to provide for ourselves and our families. We ask that you bless all those who are working hard to make a living, and may they know You value and love them. In Jesus' name, we pray. Amen.

The Eighth Beatitude

Persevering in Faith and the Promise of the Kingdom

"Blessed are those who are persecuted for righteousness' sake, for theirs is the kingdom of heaven." Matthew 5:10 (ESV)

As followers of Christ, we are called to live according to his teachings and principles, even in the face of opposition and persecution. Jesus himself warned us that the world will hate us because of him, and those who stand for righteousness will be persecuted. But even during persecution, we can take comfort in knowing that the kingdom of heaven is ours.

Check any news app, paper, or channel, and you will see daily stories about Christians being injured and their rights to worship denied. Jesus knew that not only would his followers be persecuted - and they were for centuries - but also future believers would suffer. However, he did not simply foretell persecution, he also gave us assurance that suffering will not be in vain. In this verse, Jesus blesses all who are maligned for their love of God and promises his Kingdom.

Applying the Scripture

When we encounter persecution for our faith, we should remember we are not alone. Jesus himself suffered persecution and died on the cross for us. We are called to stand firm in our faith and to continue to live according to God's principles, even when it is difficult. Remember that we have a worldwide community of Christian brothers and sisters to lean on. Reaching out to them when we struggle in persecution creates unity and strengthens us as the body of Christ. We must also remember to pray for those who persecute us, as Jesus commanded us to love our enemies and pray for those who persecute us.

Today's Prayer

Dear God, we thank you for the promise that the kingdom of heaven belongs to those who are persecuted for righteousness' sake. Help us stand firm in our faith and to live according to your principles, even in the face of opposition and persecution. Give us the strength to love our enemies and to pray for those who persecute us. May your will be done in our lives, and may we always seek to glorify you. In Jesus's name, we pray. Amen.

The Ninth Beatitude

Blessed in Persecution

※

"**B**lessed are you when others revile you and persecute you and utter all kinds of evil against you falsely on my account.Rejoice and be glad, for your reward is great in heaven, for so they persecuted the prophets who were before you." Matthew 5:11-12

※

In Matthew 5:11-12, Jesus delivers a profound message to His disciples about the inevitability of persecution and opposition as they followed Him. These verses remind us that being a follower of Christ does not exempt us from facing challenges or adversity. Instead, such challenges prepare us for the reality of living in a world that may reject or oppose truth, a struggle we witness every day.

Jesus's words in this passage offer both comfort and encouragement to those who may face persecution for their faith. He assures the disciples they are blessed when they endure persecution and slander because of their association with Him. It is a counterintuitive concept—to find a blessing in suffering—yet it echoes the often-paradoxical nature of the kingdom of God. Jesus invites His disciples, and us, to rejoice and be glad in the face of persecution. This response may seem at odds with logic and even unreasonable, but it reflects a deep trust in God's sovereignty and a confidence in the ultimate victory belonging to those who belong to Christ. As we meditate on these words, we are reminded of the lengthy line of faithful witnesses who have endured persecution throughout history. From the prophets of old to the martyrs of the early church, their examples inspire us to stand firm in our faith and to persevere in the face of opposition. For those who endure persecution for Jesus's sake, the Lord promises a glorious reward in heaven. Our present sufferings are temporary, but the rewards that await us are eternal and unfading. The reminder is that we can find our ultimate hope and security in Christ alone, not in the fleeting comforts or approval of this world.

Applying the Scripture

Today, if you face persecution or opposition because of your faith, take heart and find promise in Jesus's words. Rejoice in the privilege of being counted worthy to suffer for His name. Trust in God's faithfulness to sustain you and His promise to reward you for your faithful endurance. May we, as followers of Christ, embrace the reality of persecution with courage and faith, knowing that our ultimate reward is secure in Him. And may we find comfort in the fellowship of believers who share in our sufferings and stand together as witnesses to the transforming power of the gospel.

GOD'S LOVE IS FOREVER

Today's Prayer

Heavenly Father, thank you for the promise of blessing even in persecution. Give me the courage and strength to endure, knowing that my reward is secure in you. Help me rejoice and be glad in the face of opposition, trusting in your faithfulness to sustain me. May my lives be a testimony to your grace and truth, even amid adversity. In Jesus's name, I pray. Amen.

Letter from God

Imagine God sent you a personal letter. What would it say? How would he advise, admonish, or encourage you? In this devotion, imagine God speaking to you as he would to Jesus. And think about how this makes you feel and perhaps changes your understanding of your relationship with him.

"So, we have come to know and to believe the love that God has for us. God is love, and whoever abides in love abides in God, and God abides in him." John 4:16

My beloved child,

On this day, I want to express my love for you. You are precious to me, and my heart overflows with joy and affection as I think about you. I want you to know that I deeply cherish you, and I am not a distant or detached Father. I am intimately involved in every aspect of your life, even if you cannot see me. I have been with you from the moment you took your first breath, and I will be with you until the end of time.

My love for you knows no bounds, and my spirit is always present to comfort, guide, and protect you. Earthly fathers may fall short or disappoint you, but I am the Father whose love is always unfailing, unconditional, and unwavering. My love is not based on your performance, achievements, or failures. You can do nothing to earn or lose my love because I freely give it to you, my dear child.

You may experience pain, rejection, or brokenness in earthly relationships, but I want you to know that I will always heal and restore you. I am here to mend every piece of your broken heart and bring wholeness to your life. I bring comfort to your deepest wounds and fill the voids in your soul. You are never alone because I am always with you, holding you close in my embrace.

My child, I want to remind you of who you are. You are fearfully and wonderfully made and intricately designed. Your identity is my child, my masterpiece created with purpose, for a specific plan I will see you through. There is greatness within you because I have placed my divine imprint on you. You are the embodiment of my love and grace, and I have equipped you with the unique gifts, talents, and abilities to fulfill the calling I have placed in your life. You are not ordinary; you are extraordinary. I have given you everything you need to overcome every challenge and walk in victory. Through me, you are more than a conqueror, triumphing over every obstacle in your way. Your strength is not from your own power, but through the power of my spirit dwelling in you.

My child, strive to love others as I love you. Let your life reflect my unconditional love and grace. Extend kindness, forgiveness, and compassion to everyone around you. Be a beacon of light in a world that desperately needs to experience my love - love powerful enough to transform lives and heal broken hearts. In all you do, remember you are not alone. I am your Father, your guide, and your constant companion. I will never leave nor forsake you. Trust me with every aspect of your life. Pour out your heart to me, and I will listen. Seek my wisdom and guidance, and I will lead you on the right path.

Dearest one, remember that I love you forever, no matter what. You are the delight of my heart, and I am your strength in weakness, a guiding light in darkness, and soothing comfort in despair. Rest in my renewing love and find peace in my calming embrace. Live joyfully every day knowing that I cherish and protect you. I will always keep you safe and hold you in the palm of my hand.

With everlasting love,
   Your Father

Don't miss out!

Visit the website below and you can sign up to receive emails whenever Daniel James Duke publishes a new book. There's no charge and no obligation.

https://books2read.com/r/B-A-FIGGB-IJQAD

BOOKS 2 READ

Connecting independent readers to independent writers.

About the Author

Growing up in an Army family, Dan spent his early childhood in Florida, Germany, and Texas with his parents, brother, and sister. He enjoyed sports as a young man and continued playing softball after he joined the U.S. Air Force in 1983. His journey with the Air Force took him around the world, and his tour in Naples, Italy, deepened his appreciation of family—both spiritual and personal. It was in Naples that Dan became a deacon at a small local church of expats, immigrants, and military families. When he returned to the States, the Air Force stationed Dan in Oklahoma, where he joined a church that became his spiritual home for more than 10 years. After retirement from the Air Force, Dan relocated for work to the mid-Atlantic region of the U.S., where he currently resides. Dan also draws and paints, often gifting his works to family and friends. Dan continues his Christian leadership journey, serving as an assistant pastor and teacher for Zamar Worship Center & Ministries (https://zamarworshipctr.org/).

DELINEA PUBLISHING

About the Publisher

Delinea Publishing is an indpendent publisher of fiction and non-fiction digital and print books and digital media.

Read more at https://www.delineapublishing.com.